D1735580

How to Have a Daily Quiet Time

by
Larry Christenson

BETHANY HOUSE PUBLISHERS
MINNEAPOLIS, MINNESOTA 55438
A Division of Bethany Fellowship, Inc.

Scripture references taken from the Revised
Standard Version

How to Have a Daily Quiet Time
Larry Christenson

ISBN 0-87123-235-9

Reprinted from *The Christian Family*
A Study Guide for Groups and Individuals

Published by Bethany Fellowship, Inc.
6820 Auto Club Road, Minneapolis, Minnesota
55438

Printed in the United States of America

How to Have a Daily Quiet Time

One of Jesus' parting commands to His disciples was this: *"Make disciples of all the nations"* (Matt. 28:19). The word "disciple" comes from the same root as the word "discipline." A disciple is not just a curious or casual follower of Jesus, but a *disciplined follower.* This is what Jesus wants us to be.

To achieve something worthwhile always requires discipline. No person ever mastered a musical instrument without the discipline of regular practice. Every athlete submits to rigorous disciplines in order to excel in his chosen sport. A lawyer, doctor, housewife, mechanic, secretary, student, engineer—each must follow prescribed disciplines in order to excel. Isn't it reasonable to believe that we must also follow *spiritual disciplines* in order to excel as Christians? If we follow regular disciplines to excel in a profession, a sport, a hobby—which prepare us only for this life— shouldn't we much more follow strict disciplines which prepare us for eternity? No discipline will pay greater dividends. "The things that are seen are transient, but the things that are unseen are eternal" (2 Cor. 4:18).

The Christian religion is essentially an *experience*—a personal experience of God. Theology and doctrine are simply an explanation of that experience. Many people know something about the doctrine, but have never really had the experience. So of course their religion is dry, formal, powerless. It has no life, no zest, no sense of reality. "This is eternal life, that they might *know* thee, the only true God, and Jesus Christ whom thou hast sent" (John 17:3).

The simple discipline suggested on the next pages can change all that. It can lead you into a living experience of God. It is *a daily quiet time with God.* Every great Christian has followed a discipline similar to the one suggested here. No Christian can afford to bypass this *basic spiritual discipline.* It is gloriously simple. Yet it is astonishingly effective. We challenge you to put it into practice faithfully for *one month.* Even in that short time you will see the potential it has to literally *change your life.* "For the word of God is living and active" (Heb. 4:12).

WHAT DO I NEED?

1. A Bible.
2. A notebook (preferably a small loose-leaf which you can carry about with you).
3. A pen or pencil.
4. A quiet place.
5. A definite time set aside each day—at least 15 minutes to begin with. (It can easily grow to an hour!) The early morning is usually the best time. Make it the same time each day, whenever possible.

WHAT IS THE PROCEDURE?

1. Realize that God is with you in your quiet time. He stands ready not only to meet with you, but actually to guide and direct you. "When the Spirit of truth [the Holy Spirit] comes, he will guide you into all truth" (John 16:13). How does God come to you? He comes to you principally through His Word, the Bible. This is the

channel which the Holy Spirit uses most frequently.

2. Begin with a brief prayer. Thank God for His special blessings to you and for being here with you *now*. Tell Him that you believe—you are expecting—that He will meet with you, speak to you, and reveal His will to you through this quiet time. "You will seek me and find me; when you seek me with all your heart, I will be found by you, says the Lord" (Jer. 29:13, 14).

3. Read the brief passage of Scripture which you have chosen for the day.

   a. Do not read simply to "understand." Read with a feeling of "openness" and "receptivity." You are "feeding" on God's Word. It is spiritual food to you. "Man shall not live by bread alone, but by every word that proceeds from the mouth of God" (Matt. 4:4).

   b. You will not understand everything you read. Don't let that bother you. Take it in. Whisper to God, "I don't get all of this . . . but I know that You will help me to understand as we move along." "The fear [reverence] of the Lord is the beginning of knowledge" (Prov. 1:7).

   c. Let your reading be broken up by moments of prayer and meditation. In other words, *enjoy* this spiritual meal. Taste it. Savor it. Read parts of it out loud to hear how it sounds with differing emphases.

4. Write down what comes to you during this reading-meditating-praying time. THIS IS THE KEY TO YOUR WHOLE QUIET TIME. When you write down, you begin to crystalize and capture the actual workings of the Holy Spirit in your heart, mind, and soul. Make it quite personal and direct. Not simply what the passage "means," but what it means *to and for you.* Perhaps it will trigger some thought not directly related to the passage you are reading. That's all right. Write it down. *This is the Holy Spirit's personal message to you.*

   a. Naturally you are not always "tuned in" to the Holy Spirit 100 percent—you will get some "static" from your own thoughts and opinions. But more and more, *as you faithfully follow this daily discipline*, your little notebook will become a record of God's personal dealing with your own life.

   b. Here is an actual sample of someone's quiet time record for one day: "June 3rd. The Lord's Prayer. The Apostles'

Creed. Romans 6:22-23. Now that I am set free from sin and become a slave of God, my return is sanctification and its end, eternal life. For the wages of sin is death, but the free gift of God is eternal life in Christ Jesus, our Lord. It's a good feeling to rid ourselves of sin, to feel clean and in God's good graces everlastingly. How can we know and learn of God without the will to do so? This I think of so much of late. But what joy it brings to know we have our heavenly Father, our living God, to go to. We give thanks to Thee, yes, more than thanks, O Lord our God, for all Thy goodness. Amen."

5. Close with a time of prayer.

   a. Begin with thanks, praise, adoration.

   b. Confess your sins, asking God's forgiveness.

   c. Affirm your faith in God. Say at least several strong statements of faith. For example—"God is my refuge and strength! . . . I know that Jesus Christ is alive, and His Kingdom is surely coming; it will come to me today! . . . I can do all things through Christ who strengthens me! . . . With God nothing shall be impossible! . . . The Lord is my shepherd! . . . He leadeth me, O blessed thought!"

d. Present to God your petitions and requests. You may want to keep a prayer-list, and check them off as God answers them. Don't be satisfied with unanswered prayer. Jesus said, "Whatever you ask in prayer, believe that you are receiving it and you will" (Mark 11:24). Keep the list small enough so you can pray for each need with real purpose and faith.

OTHER POINTS

1. A Daily Quiet Time with God is one spiritual discipline—one of the most important—but still only one. If your life as a Christian is to mature in a healthy way, you will want to observe other basic disciplines as well. These can be carried out most effectively within the framework of your own local church:

a. Regular church attendance.

b. Regular Bible study under a qualified Bible teacher.

c. Regular giving to the Lord's work (ten percent of your income).

    d. Regular work or service for the Lord under the supervision of those placed over you in the Lord.

2. Divide your notebook into two sections. The first section is to record your Daily Quiet Time. In the second section you take notes on sermons, lectures, Bible studies, radio talks, thoughts that come to you during the day—anything of spiritual value. In order to integrate these notes into your life in a practical way, convert them into a prayer during your next quiet time. In other words, take the substance of the notes and boil it down into a prayer. Apply it to your own life.

WHERE SHOULD I START IN THE BIBLE?

1. One of the simplest methods for selecting your daily Bible passage is to read through a single book, a few verses each day. The Gospel of John, Colossians, the Epistle of James, and the First Epistle of John are good ones to begin with.

2. You may want to follow certain themes, such as salvation, forgiveness, healing, etc. If so, use a Bible concordance to find different passages dealing with your theme.

3. Another way to begin would be to use the following series of Bible passages, which will lead you through some basic Christian teachings in a systematic way. Some can be covered in a single day; others might be worth spending several days on:

   a. The "new life" of a Christian: 1 John 5:9-13; James 1:2-8; James 1:19-26; 1 John 1:5-10; Mark 8:34-38; Eph. 2:1-10; 1 Pet. 1:3-9; 1 Pet. 1:22-2:3; John 15:1-11; 2 Cor. 5:14-21.

   b. Christian responsibility: Phil. 4:4-13; 1 Pet. 3:8-17; Rom. 14:13-23; Col. 3:16-25; Gal. 6:1-10.

   c. Adventuring in the Psalms: Psalms 1, 8, 73, 32, 46, 139, 91, 22.